Contents

English

Maths

Science

Published by CGP

ISBN: 978 1 78294 204 7

Contains public sector information licensed under the Open Government Licence v2.0.
http://www.nationalarchives.gov.uk/doc/open-government-licence/

www.cgpbooks.co.uk
Printed by Elanders Ltd, Newcastle upon Tyne.

Clipart from Corel®

English

Reading — Word Reading	🙁	🙂
I can use my knowledge of phonic rules to spell and pronounce words so that I can read fluently.		
I can read accurately by blending sounds in words that include graphemes I have been taught, especially graphemes which represent more than one sound.		
I can read words with multiple syllables containing graphemes I have been taught, especially graphemes which represent more than one sound.		
I can read words containing common suffixes.		
I can read an increasing number of words that are common exceptions to spelling rules, and I can identify unusual relationships between letters and sounds.		
I can read most words with speed and accuracy, without needing to blend the sounds of familiar words aloud.		
I can read books aloud when the words follow phonic rules I have been taught, and I can sound out unfamiliar words correctly and quickly.		
I can reread books to increase my fluency and confidence.		

Reading — Comprehension	🙁	🙂
I can listen to, discuss and express views on a range of contemporary and classic poetry, fiction and non-fiction that is above the level that I can read on my own.		
I can describe the order of events in a book and how information is related.		
I have read and can retell an increasing number of stories, fairy stories and traditional tales.		
I have been introduced to non-fiction texts with different structures.		
I can identify simple recurring literary language in stories and poetry.		

Reading — Comprehension (cont.)	😐	😊
I can discuss word meanings, linking words I already know to new words.		
I can talk to other people about my favourite words and phrases.		
I know and enjoy an increasing number of poems and can recite some of these out loud by heart, using intonation effectively.		
I can use my own knowledge, or information and vocabulary provided by my teacher, to understand books I read or hear.		
I can check that a text makes sense as I read, and correct any errors in my reading.		
I can infer meanings from what characters say and do.		
I can ask and answer questions about the books I have read and heard.		
I can predict what might happen next in a story based on what I have already read or heard.		
I can take part in discussions about books that I have read and those that have been read to me, and listen to other people's opinions about them.		
I can explain my understanding of books I have read and those that have been read to me.		

Writing — Transcription	😐	😊
I can spell many words correctly by breaking spoken words into sounds and using the correct letters to represent these sounds.		
I have learnt new ways of spelling sounds which have several alternative spellings, including words containing each spelling, and some common homophones.		
I can spell words that are common exceptions to the spelling rules I know.		
I can spell an increasing number of contractions.		
I can use an apostrophe for singular noun possession.		

4

Writing — Transcription (cont.)	😐	😊
I can tell the difference between a homophone and a near-homophone.		
I can add suffixes to form longer words, including 'ment', 'ness', 'ful', 'less' and 'ly'.		
I can apply the spelling rules I have been taught to words I write.		
I can write simple sentences correctly from dictation, including words that follow spelling rules, common exceptions and punctuation I have been taught.		

Writing — Handwriting	😐	😊
I can write lower-case letters of the correct size compared to one another.		
I have started to use diagonal and horizontal strokes to join adjacent letters, and I understand when this is appropriate.		
I can write capital letters and digits of the correct size and relationship to one another and lower-case letters.		
I can use spacing between words that is appropriate for the size of letters.		

Writing — Composition	😐	😊
I can write fictional and true stories about my own and others' experiences.		
I can write about real events.		
I can write poetry.		
I can produce writing for different purposes.		
I can plan and explain out loud what I am going to write.		

Writing — Composition (cont.)	😐	🙂
I can note down ideas, words and vocabulary to use in my writing.		
I can summarise what I am going to write, and break it down into sentences.		
I can evaluate my writing with my teacher and other pupils.		
I can reread my writing to check it makes sense and that verbs, including continuous verbs, are consistently in the correct tense.		
I can check a piece of writing for spelling, grammar and punctuation errors.		
I can read what I have written out loud, using intonation to make my meaning clear.		

Writing — Vocabulary, Grammar and Punctuation	😐	🙂
I can use new and familiar punctuation correctly, including full stops, capital letters, exclamation marks, question marks, commas for lists, apostrophes for contractions and apostrophes for singular noun possession.		
I can write statements, questions, exclamations and commands.		
I can use expanded noun phrases for descriptions and to be specific.		
I can use the present and past tense correctly and consistently, including the progressive form.		
I can use subordinating and co-ordinating conjunctions correctly in sentences.		
I can use the grammar rules I have been taught.		
I understand some features of written Standard English.		
I can use the grammatical terms that I have been taught to talk about my writing.		

Spoken Language	😐	😊
I can listen and respond appropriately to adults and other people my age.		
I can ask relevant questions to increase my understanding and knowledge.		
I have used different ways to expand my vocabulary.		
I can explain and justify my own answers, arguments and opinions.		
I can describe, explain and narrate for different purposes in a structured way, including expressing feelings.		
I can pay attention and take part in conversations with others, staying on topic and making and responding to comments.		
I can use spoken language to suggest ideas and explanations, and to explore my imagination and ideas.		
I can speak clearly and fluently, increasingly using Standard English.		
I can take part in discussions, presentations, performances, role play, improvisations and debates.		
I can gain, keep and monitor the interest of people listening to me.		
I can assess different viewpoints and build on other people's contributions.		
I can choose and use appropriate registers (e.g. formal or informal speaking) to communicate effectively.		

Teacher Comments

Maths

Number and Place Value	😐	😊
I can recognise the place value of each digit in a two-digit number.		
I can read and write numbers up to at least 100 in numerals and words.		
I can count forwards and backwards in steps of 2, 3, 5 and 10.		
I can find, show and estimate numbers on a number line.		
I can use partitioning to show numbers in different ways.		
I can compare and order numbers from 0 to 100.		
I can use greater than (>), less than (<) and equals (=) signs to compare and order numbers.		
I can solve problems using the things I've learned about numbers.		

Calculations	😐	😊
I can solve addition and subtraction problems that involve numbers, quantities and measures.		
I can solve addition and subtraction problems using objects, pictures and mental maths.		
I know the number bonds up to 100 and can use number facts to answer questions.		
I can add and subtract a two-digit number and ones.		
I can add and subtract a two digit number and tens.		
I can add and subtract two two-digit numbers.		

Calculations (cont.)	😐	🙂
I can add three one-digit numbers.		
I know that subtraction of one number from another must be done in order, but addition can be done in any order.		
I know adding and subtracting are opposites and can use this to check my answers and solve missing number problems.		
I know the 2, 5 and 10 times tables and their division facts.		
I can recognise odd and even numbers.		
I know that dividing one number by another must be done in order, but multiplication can be done in any order.		
I can solve multiplication and division problems, including problems in contexts, using different methods.		
I can write and use mathematical statements using the multiplication (×), division (÷) and equals (=) signs.		

Fractions	😐	🙂
I can recognise and find simple fractions (thirds and quarters) of lengths, shapes, sets of objects and quantities.		
I can work out simple fractions of whole numbers.		
I can recognise simple equivalent fractions.		

Measurement	😐	🙂
I can estimate length, height, mass, volume and temperature using the correct units.		
I can use the right tools to measure length, height, mass, volume and temperature.		

Measurement (cont.)	😐	😊
I can compare and order length, mass and volume using less than (<), greater than (>) and equals (=).		
I can use pounds (£) and pence (p) to make up different amounts of money.		
I can find different combinations of coins that make up the same amount of money.		
I can add and subtract to solve simple money problems, including giving change.		
I can write and tell the time to five minutes, and draw hands on a clock face to show time.		
I can compare different lengths of time.		
I know the number of minutes in an hour and the number of hours in a day.		

Geometry	😐	😊
I can pick out and describe 2D shapes, including the number of sides and lines of symmetry.		
I can pick out and describe 3D shapes, including the number of edges, vertices and faces.		
I can pick out 2D shapes on the surface of 3D shapes.		
I can compare and sort 2D shapes and 3D shapes and everyday objects.		
I can recognise and make patterns and sequences out of shapes.		
I can use mathematical terms to describe position and movement.		
I know what a right angle turn is (clockwise and anticlockwise), and how many are in a quarter, half and three-quarter turn.		

Statistics	😐	🙂
I can draw and use simple tables.		
I can draw and use tally charts.		
I can draw and use block diagrams.		
I can draw and use pictograms.		
I can ask and answer questions by counting the objects in a category and sorting categories by quantity.		
I can ask and answer questions about totalling and comparing data in categories.		

Teacher Comments

Science

Living Things and their Habitats	😐	😊
I can compare the differences between things that are living, dead, and things that have never been alive.		
I know that most living things are suited to the habitats that they live in.		
I know how different habitats provide for the basic needs of different kinds of plants and animals.		
I understand how plants and animals in a habitat depend on each other to survive.		
I can identify some common plants and animals in their habitats.		
I can use simple food chains to describe how animals get their food from plants and other animals.		

Plants	😐	😊
I can describe how seeds and bulbs grow into fully-grown plants.		
I know that plants need water, light and a suitable temperature to grow and be healthy.		

Animals, including Humans	😐	😊
I know that humans and other animals have children which grow into adults.		
I know that humans and animals need water, food and air to live.		
I know that humans need to exercise, eat the right amounts of different foods and have good hygiene to be healthy.		

Uses of Everyday Materials	😐	😊
I can identify objects that are made out of wood, metal, plastic, glass, brick, rock, paper and cardboard.		
I can compare different materials and say which is best for a particular use.		
I know how the shape of objects made of some materials can be squashed, bent, twisted or stretched.		

The following statements cover the Programme of Study for Years 1 and 2.
Some of the statements may have been covered in Year 1.

Working Scientifically	😐	😊
I can ask simple scientific questions.		
I know that it may be possible to answer scientific questions in different ways.		
I can make observations using simple equipment.		
I can carry out simple tests to answer scientific questions.		
I can identify and classify different plants, animals, materials and objects.		
I can gather and record data to help answer questions.		
I can use my observations and ideas to suggest answers to questions.		

Teacher Comments

Naturally bonkers

ISBN 978 1 78294 204 7

9 781782 942047

SME2P11   £2.00
                 (Retail Price)

www.cgpbooks.co.uk

Name: .... Teacher: .... Class: ....

Key Stage One
English • Maths • Science

Year **2**

Pupil Progress Booklet